MYSTERIES OF
THE UNIVERSE

Light

JIM WHITING

CREATIVE EDUCATION

Published by Creative Education
P.O. Box 227, Mankato, Minnesota 56002
Creative Education is an imprint of The Creative Company
www.thecreativecompany.us

Design and production by Blue Design
Art direction by Rita Marshall
Printed in the United States of America

Photographs by Getty Images (Franz Aberham, Apic, Harry Bartlett,
Skip Brown, Alan Copson, George Diebold Photography, Hulton Archive,
Nathan Lazarnick/George Eastman House, Ottavio Mario Leoni,
MILpictures by Tom Weber, Kyu Oh, Science Picture Co, SSPL, Dimitri
Vervitsiotis), NASA (JAXA/NASA, NASA, NASA/JPL-Caltech/UCLA,
NASA/SDO)

Cover and folio illustration © 2011 Alex Ryan

Library of Congress Cataloging-in-Publication Data
Whiting, Jim.
Light / by Jim Whiting.
p. cm. — (Mysteries of the universe)
Includes bibliographical references and index.
Summary: An examination of the science behind the physical
phenomenon known as light, including relevant theories and history-
making discoveries as well as topics of current and future research.
ISBN 978-1-60818-190-2
1. Light—Juvenile literature. I. Title.

QC360.W46 2012
535—dc23   2011040143

First Edition
9 8 7 6 5 4 3 2 1

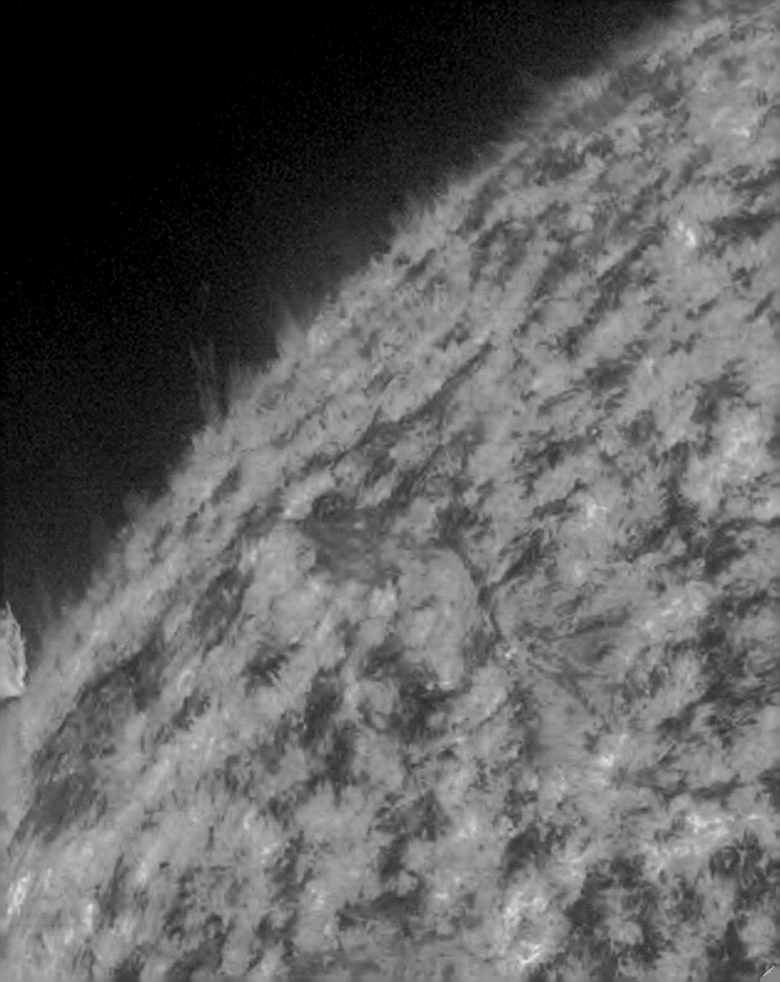

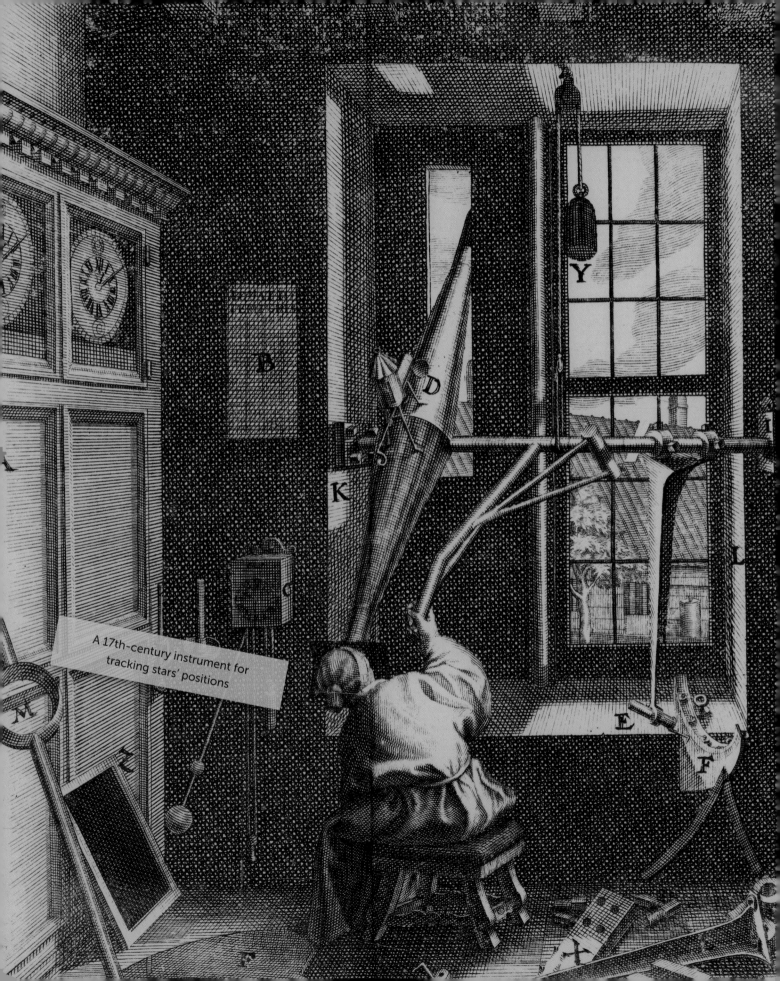

A 17th-century instrument for tracking stars' positions

TABLE OF CONTENTS

INTRODUCTION 9

CHAPTERS

LET THERE BE LIGHT 10

FROM LEGENDS TO LASERS 17

REVEALING SOME OF THE MYSTERIES 29

THE FUTURE OF LIGHT 37

LIGHT ASIDES

CAMERA OBSCURA GOES DIGITAL 21

INSIDE THE GAME 27

THE NAME IS BOND—LASER BOND 41

A BETTER WAY OF LIGHTING? 44

ENDNOTES 46

WEB SITES 47

SELECTED BIBLIOGRAPHY 47

INDEX 48

The lights of Earth's cities can be seen from space

INTRODUCTION

For most of human history, the true nature of the universe was shrouded in myth and mystery. About 400 years ago, scientists began unraveling those mysteries. Their efforts were so successful that American **physicist** Albert Michelson wrote in 1894, "The more important fundamental laws and facts of physical science have all been discovered, and these are now so firmly established that the possibility of their ever being supplemented in consequence of new discoveries is exceedingly remote." William Thomson, Baron Kelvin, perhaps that era's most famous physicist, echoed Michelson: "There is nothing new to be discovered in physics now. All that remains is more and more precise measurement." Both men were wrong. Within a few years, scientists had revealed the makeup of the tiny **atom** and the unexpected vastness of outer space. Yet the universe doesn't yield its mysteries easily, and much remains to be discovered.

Some of these discoveries will necessarily involve light. Light affects every aspect of our lives from the moment we awake to the time we go to sleep. Yet, for many years, humans were in the dark when it came to knowledge about the nature of light. Now we know many of its properties, its incredible speed, and even how to create it, literally turning night into day. However, there are still things about light that puzzle us. And we are just beginning to understand how to harness its awesome potential to both improve life on Earth and explore the heavens.

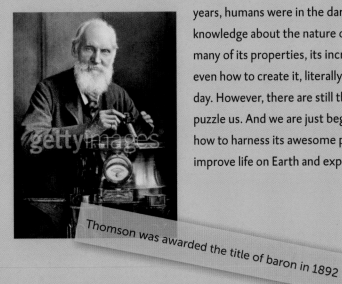

Thomson was awarded the title of baron in 1892

LET THERE BE LIGHT

Light is essential to the survival of all life on Earth. A world of perpetual darkness would be a world in which nothing happened, nothing grew, and nothing lived. As humans, we have five senses that detect the presence of things around us. Not all the senses are equally effective. Touch and taste work only when we are next to an object. Smell extends our knowledge a little farther. Hearing casts an even wider net.

Yet there's little question that sight is our most vital sense. Imagine yourself as an early human. Sight would allow you to see prey from miles away and thereby take steps to provide yourself with the nourishment you need to survive. It would also let you see predators that want to make a meal of you soon enough to escape.

Sight depends on light. In their book *Life: An Introduction to Biology*, **paleontologist** George G. Simpson and **hematologist** William S. Beck conclude that "as a stimulus for giving information about the environment, light is in a class by itself in the amount of information it can give and in giving information about things at a distance from the organism [living thing]." Light enables us to interpret what we see and gives meaning to that information.

Although we get light from electricity, the stars, fires such as campfires and candles, and even insects such as fireflies and glowworms, the sun is by far our most important source of light. (We may think of moonlight as well, but that is only sunlight that bounces off the moon and is reflected onto Earth.) **Astronomers** believe that the sun is about 4.6 billion years old and that it will last at least that much longer.

What is sunlight? It was a mystery for most of recorded history, but within the past four centuries scientists have discovered more about it and agreed on many aspects, including the fundamental nature of how it works. The sun acts like a gigantic power plant, sending out vast amounts of **radiation**. This radiation takes the form of **electromagnetic waves** that bathe Earth at every moment.

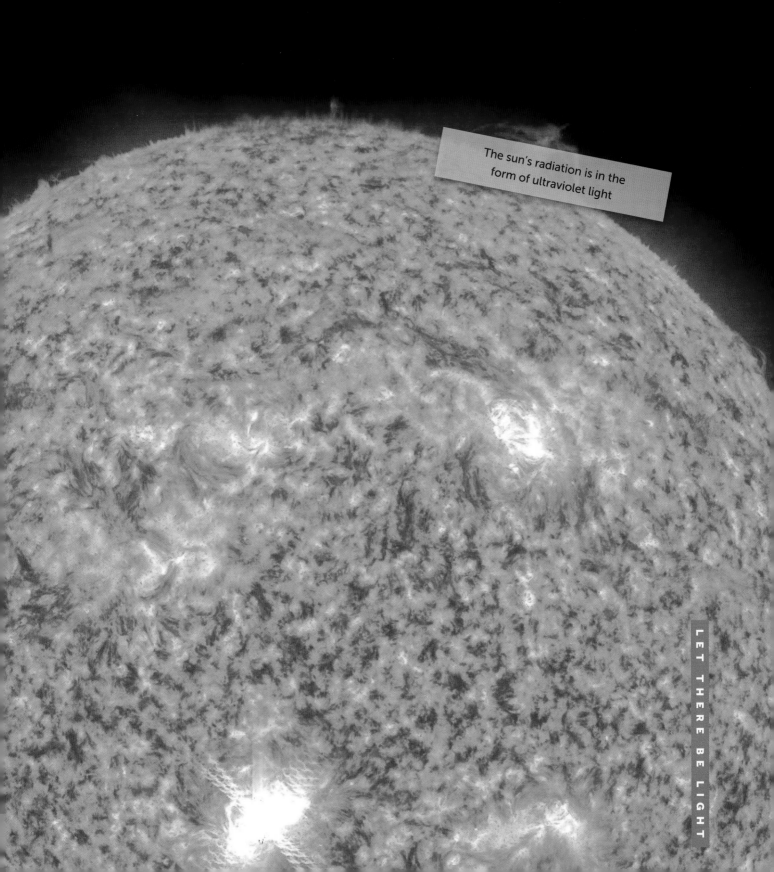

The sun's radiation is in the form of ultraviolet light

LET THERE BE LIGHT

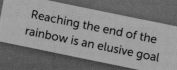

Reaching the end of the rainbow is an elusive goal

We're familiar with waves from watching water in oceans and lakes—and even in swimming pools and bathtubs. We think of them as being in motion. In reality, though, the water doesn't move. Rather, the apparent motion comes from energy initiated by the wind that travels through the water. The size of any wave—whether oceanic or electromagnetic—is measured by the distance between either the tops of successive waves (called peaks) or the bottoms (troughs). In the **electromagnetic spectrum**, these distances can range from several miles for the longest (**radio waves**) to 0.1–0.000001 **nanometers** (nm) for the shortest (**gamma rays**). The shorter the wavelength, the more energy the waves contain.

Visible light—light we use to see the world around us—extends over a tiny portion of this spectrum, making up perhaps one-thousandth of one percent. Its wavelengths vary from about 400 to 700 nm. This variation arises because sunlight, though white in appearance, is a mixture of seven different colors, each with its own wavelength (from longest to shortest): red, orange, yellow, green, blue, indigo, and violet. These colors appear distinctly in soap bubbles, drops of water, **prisms**, and—perhaps most spectacularly—rainbows. As American physics professor Gary Waldman notes about rainbows, "all the light of a single color is coming from one *angle* rather than one *position* in space. This nonlocalized property is why you can never reach the mythical pot of gold at the end of the rainbow; if you move in that direction, new raindrops farther away than the original ones will be sending you the colored light."

Other wavelengths close to the visible spectrum are detectable under certain conditions. The next longest wavelength beyond the visible spectrum is infrared light (700–100,000 nm), which is given off by anything with body heat. Night-vision goggles allow us to "see" infrared light. Snakes such as pit vipers can also form a "picture" of their prey by sensing their infrared radiation.

On the opposite side of visible light (50–400 nm) is ultraviolet (UV), which some

Gas lamps were used both outdoors and indoors before electricity

birds and bees are capable of seeing but which is invisible to humans. Crime scene investigators use portable UV "flashlights" to spot traces of blood that have been washed off a surface. UV light from the sun produces vitamin D, an essential element in bone growth. On the other hand, too much exposure to UV light produces sunburn or even cancer. X-rays (0.1–20 nm) have even shorter wavelengths than UV light. Medical professionals use X-ray machines to see under their patients' skin and detect conditions such as broken bones and brain tumors.

When we look at an object, it appears to be one (or a combination of several) of the seven basic colors. Actually, an object reflects that color while absorbing the others. Thus an orange reflects orange light, a stop sign reflects red light, and a lemon reflects yellow light. Plants that look green to us because they reflect green light contain a substance called chlorophyll. Chlorophyll is present in all living things that go through a process called photosynthesis, in which plants and other organisms use light energy from the sun to make the sugars they need for growth.

Another characteristic of light makes the sky appear blue. As sunlight enters Earth's atmosphere, it strikes air **molecules**. These collisions cause the light to scatter. Colors with longer wavelengths (such as red and orange) aren't as affected by the collisions as ones with shorter wavelengths, especially blue, which may be scattered multiple times. So no matter the direction in which you look, the sky appears to be blue. At sunset, sunlight has to travel much farther in the atmosphere to reach your eyes. The blue scattering increases so much that the color almost disappears, leaving primarily the reds, oranges, and yellows that can make the sky seem as if it's on fire.

Today we are accustomed to flipping a switch at home, at school, or at work and instantly having light. This isn't surprising, since light travels at a speed of 186,282 miles (299,792 km) per second. If someone were standing five miles (8 km) away and turned on a light, it would seem instantaneous to us. Light travels far faster than sound—nearly 875,000 times as fast. If that same person shouted something through an amplifying device such as a megaphone, we wouldn't hear any sound for nearly 24 seconds.

It's only when we look upward into the heavens that light seems to slow down. It takes light about eight minutes to travel from the sun to Earth. When we get to the stars, the distances light has to travel become so vast that writing down numbers with a bunch of zeros becomes almost meaningless. Toward the end of the 19th century, astronomers adopted the concept of light years, the distance that light travels in a year, and found it to be just under 6 trillion miles (9.4607×10^{12} km).

The closest star to Earth—other than our sun—is Proxima Centauri, which is 4.2 light years away, or about 24 trillion miles (40 trillion km). Other stars in the night sky are even farther away. The Andromeda **galaxy**, which we can see from Earth with the aid of telescopes, still is a staggering 2.5 million light years away! In the farthest reaches of the universe, there are stars that we haven't even seen because their light is still traveling toward us.

LET THERE BE LIGHT

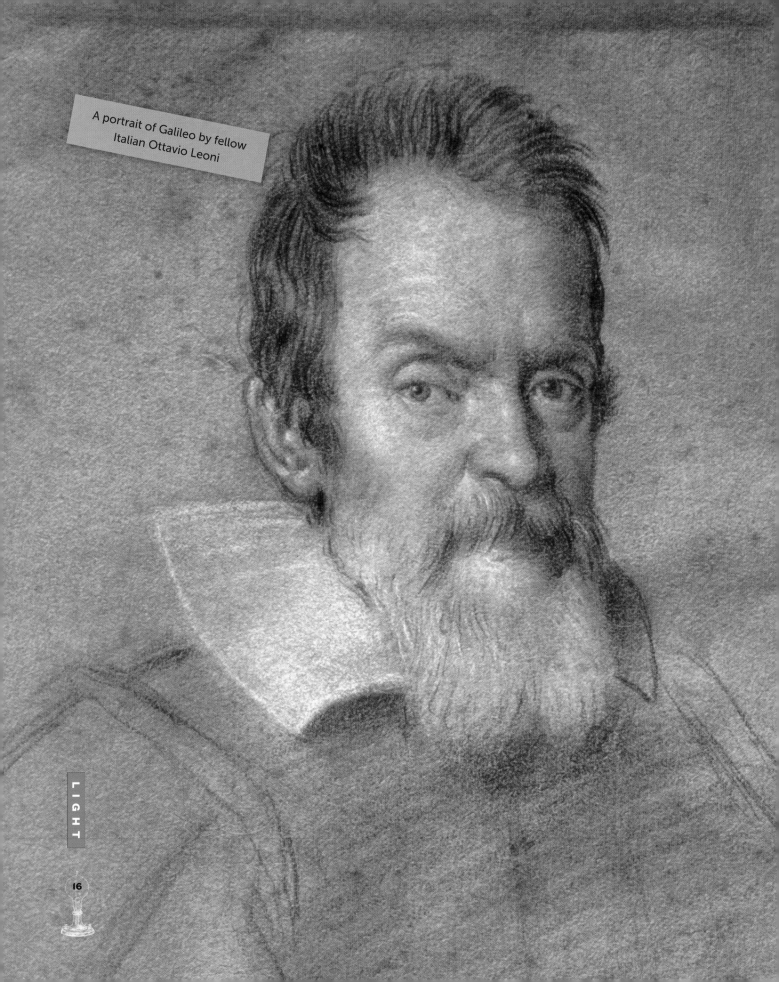

A portrait of Galileo by fellow Italian Ottavio Leoni

BLACK HOLES

ENERGY

GALAXIES

GRAVITY

LIGHT

MYSTERIES OF
THE UNIVERSE

MASS & MATTER

SPACE & TIME

STARS

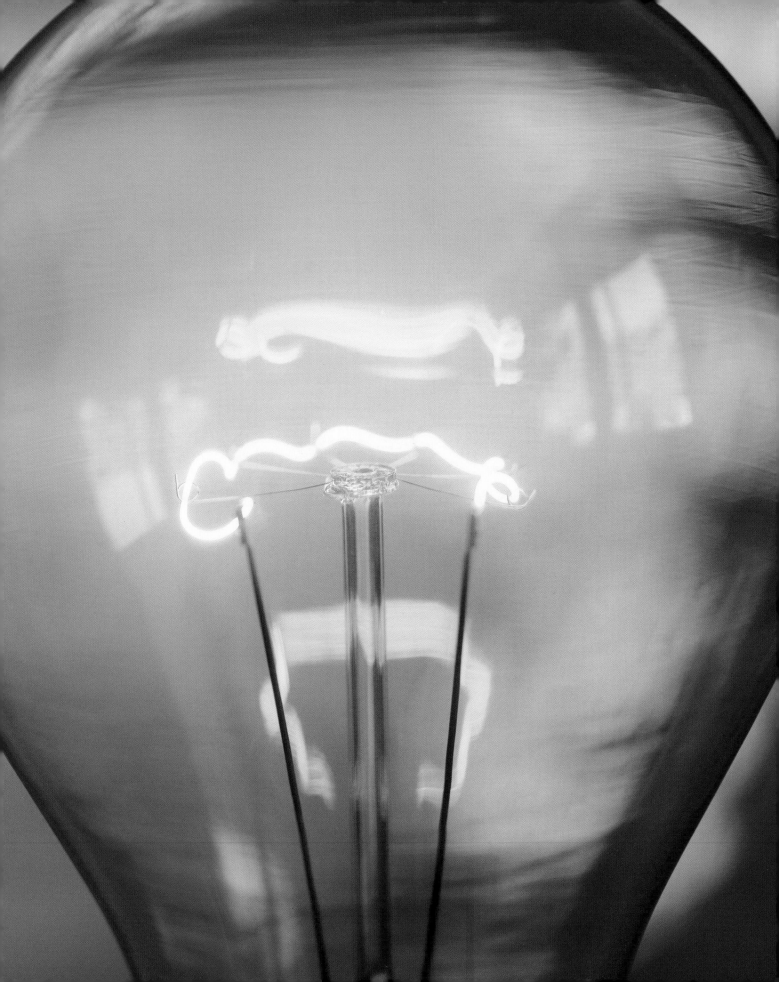

FROM LEGENDS TO LASERS

Light was a great mystery to the ancients. All they knew was that the sun came up every morning and bathed Earth in light and heat. It slowly made its way across the sky and eventually disappeared, leaving them in darkness until the process repeated itself the following day.

Because of the sun's vital importance, many ancient cultures—such as the Egyptians, Mayans, and Greeks—worshiped it and made it one of their most important gods. Some went even further, connecting the sun's power to human rulers. For instance, the Japanese believed that their legendary first emperor Jimmu—and all his successors—was descended from Amaterasu, the sun goddess.

Although the sun was the most important source of light to the ancients, fire wasn't far behind. No one knows how or when humans discovered fire-making, though archaeological evidence points to a time period as long as 500,000 years ago. Firelight pushed back the terrors of the night because people could see after the sun went down. They began experimenting with other ways of creating light. One of the first successes was the early oil lamp, which can be traced back to about 8000 B.C. and burned animal fat and oils from plants. Then came candles, which date back at least to biblical times.

Starting in the sixth century B.C., ancient Greek thinkers began seeking what today we might call scientific explanations of light and vision. Some of them theorized that beams of light came from within the eyes of people and touched distant objects. This process enabled them to see those objects, though it was unclear how the beams originated. The Greeks also turned their attention to the speed of light. Most thought this speed was infinite, or limitless, though a few maintained that it was finite and thus able to be measured. Neither side had any way of making measurements, so there was no way of backing up their opinions. The debate continued into the early 1600s A.D., when Italian physicist and astronomer Galileo Galilei attempted some crude experiments to measure light's speed. While he could conclude only that it was more than 10 times faster than the speed of sound, Galileo opened the floodgates with his willingness to conduct experiments. Other scientists followed his lead. Unlike in earlier eras, they now used experimental data to support their respective positions.

n many situations, breakthroughs in scientific knowledge don't make it past the notice of other scientists in the field. That has not been the case with the study of light, where more knowledge has often led to practical applications benefiting many people. For example, the principle of **refraction** made the invention of eyeglasses possible. Refraction is immediately obvious to anyone who puts a stick or other object into water. The underwater part of the stick appears to bend, but the bending is an **optical**

Reflective surfaces such as water mirror light's effects

A camera obscura from around the 1860s

Camera Obscura Goes Digital

Nearly 1,000 years ago, an Arab scientist named Alhazen showed that admitting sunlight through a tiny pinhole in the wall of a room produced images of landscapes, buildings, and even people on the opposite wall. These images accurately reflected the color and perspective of the subject, and artists could trace the outlines. Several centuries later, this technique was termed camera obscura, from Latin words for "dark chamber." Eventually the size of the camera was reduced to a large box with a screen inside. Artists could carry it with them anywhere they went. In the 1800s, people began to experiment with making permanent images. They put paper coated with light-sensitive chemicals on the side opposite the pinhole. They exposed the paper to light through the pinhole for hours, thereby producing dim images. They called this process "photography," which means "writing with light." Advances in cameras and film soon opened up photography to millions of people. But the film had to be developed using special chemicals and then printed. Today, digital photography eliminates the need for time-consuming development by using electronic sensors rather than light-sensitive film to record images of the scene being photographed. Photographers can immediately view the results, and the art of writing with light lives on.

illusion. As light beams pass through a glass lens, they are refracted, or bent, and converge at a point behind the lens. This bending of light produces clearer images of the outside world and improves the lens wearer's vision.

Early lens makers also used their skills to uncover worlds that had previously gone unnoticed. The first optical microscope appeared in the Netherlands in 1590 and enabled viewers to see a strange new realm of tiny creatures. Fewer than 20 years later, a Dutch lens maker named Hans Lippershey discovered that a combination of lenses in a long tube magnified faraway objects. Galileo learned of Lippershey's invention and built an improved version of the device, soon called a telescope. He used it to make startling discoveries that began to help explain the structure of the universe and provide even

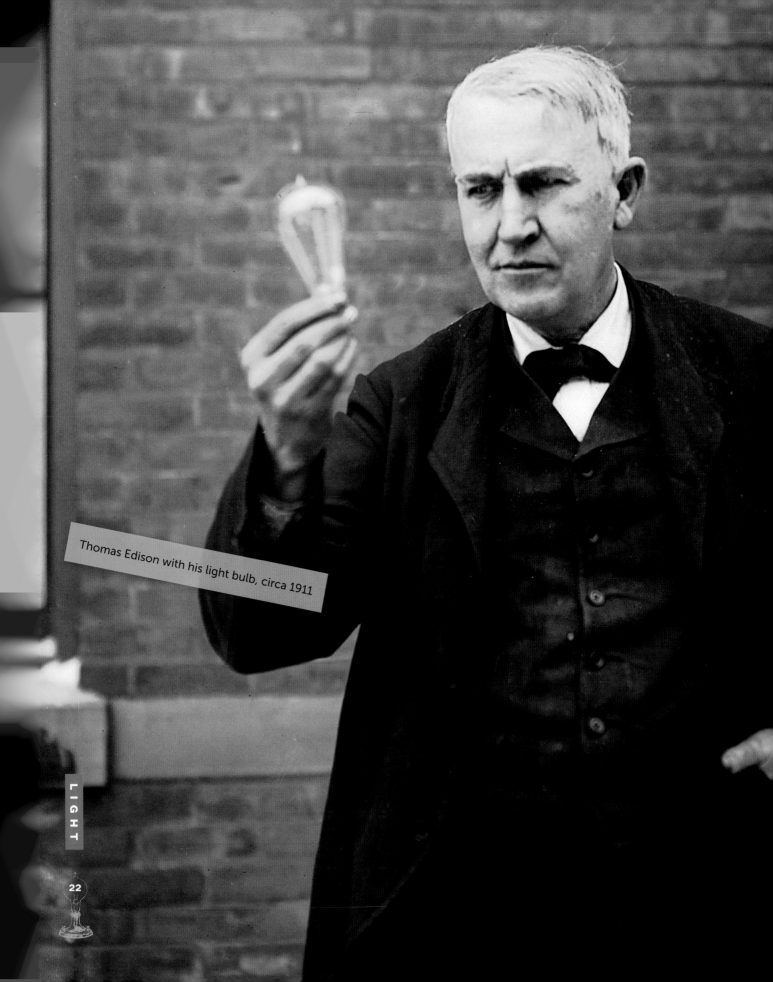

Thomas Edison with his light bulb, circa 1911

more information about the properties of light. Today, the Hubble Space Telescope gives us some of the most striking images ever taken in outer space.

One of the great advances in light technology came late in the 1800s when American inventor Thomas Edison produced the first commercially successful incandescent light bulb. A bulb produces light because an electric current heats a filament inside the bulb, causing the filament to glow. Edison tested hundreds of filament materials to find one that would last as long as possible without melting or bursting into flames. Eventually he settled on a carbon-based thread, though today a metal called tungsten is the most common filament material.

The advent of fluorescent light early in the 20th century offered new possibilities. This lighting is normally produced in thin glass tubes containing a small amount of mercury, a silvery metal found in liquid form, and a gas such as neon. An electric current passes into the tube, stimulating the mercury and changing it from a liquid to a gas. This process makes UV light, which we can't see. The tube is coated with white phosphor salt, a substance that produces visible light when exposed to UV light. Fluorescent light fixtures create less heat than incandescent bulbs and last longer, but the tubes are more expensive to produce, and the mercury presents a difficulty in disposal because it is hazardous to the environment.

In the late 1950s, laser light was developed. "Laser" is an **acronym** that stands for "light amplification by stimulated emission of radiation." To produce laser light, an electric current is introduced into a tube containing a material, which can be a solid, gas, or liquid. The current quickly stimulates the atoms of the laser material into producing light, which varies in intensity according to the material being used. Mirrors at each end of the tube bounce the light back and forth, creating increasingly higher levels of intensity. Soon it becomes so intense and powerful that it bursts from one end of the tube.

One reason for this intensity is that laser light consists of a single wavelength rather than the mixture of wavelengths found in ordinary white light. It is also "coherent," meaning that its peaks and troughs are perfectly aligned. As American **science fiction** author and science writer Ben Bova explains, "ordinary light sources produce light waves of many different types, all jumbled together like an auditorium full of freewheeling rock dancers. Lasers produce light waves that are more precisely spaced and lined up than a marching squad of West Point cadets."

While this process of producing laser light may sound complicated and time-consuming, it isn't. It takes only a few millionths of a second. The result is very different

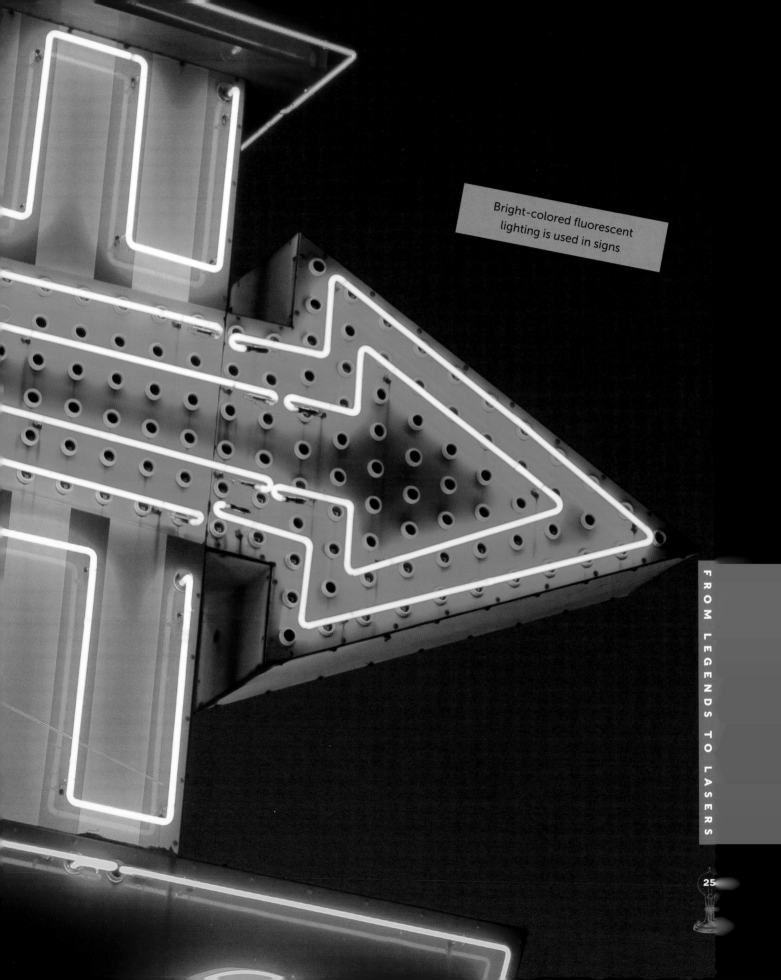

Bright-colored fluorescent lighting is used in signs

Optical fibers are often wrapped in bundles

Inside the Game

Light plays an important role in the 1982 film *Tron*, one of the first movies to make extensive use of computer animation. Much of the movie's action centers on the laser laboratory of a corporation called ENCOM. The main character, a hacker named Kevin Flynn (played by Jeff Bridges), has created several computer codes. A rival, Ed Dillinger, steals Flynn's work and presents it as his own. Aided by his girlfriend and another ENCOM employee, Alan Bradley (played by Bruce Boxleitner), Flynn tries to reveal Dillinger's dishonesty. But Dillinger has Master Control Program (MCP), a large-scale artificial intelligence program, on his side. MCP uses a laser beam to digitize Flynn and send him into a potentially lethal computer game that features light cycles. These resemble motorcycles and produce walls of light as they roar around the game grid. Cycles hitting the walls are eliminated from the game. Flynn and Tron (a security program designed by Bradley to combat MCP) escape from the game. They undergo numerous adventures as MCP and its allies pursue them, with Flynn also trying to return to the real world. The film developed a cult following over the years and generated several computer games and comic books. In December 2010, a sequel titled *Tron: Legacy* was released.

from ordinary light, though. For example, if you shine a flashlight against a wall, the light immediately disperses and covers a large space. Laser light remains a narrow, tightly focused beam. It is so focused that it was even used to measure the distance from Earth to the moon. In 1962, scientists from the Massachusetts Institute of Technology (MIT) conducted a project called "Luna See." They used a telescope to send a laser beam to the moon and "clocked" the amount of time it took the beam to return. The result was the most accurate reading of the distance ever obtained.

Lasers also opened up a much faster and more efficient way of communicating. Copper wires, traditionally the most common way of transmitting telephone signals, are limited in the amount of information they can carry. In 1970, the first practical optical fibers were invented. One-tenth the thickness of a human hair, optical fibers can transmit at least 10 times the information normally encoded on copper wire. Further improvements will allow them to become even more powerful in the future.

Dutch astronomer and mathematician Christiaan Huygens, circa 1670

REVEALING SOME OF THE MYSTERIES

The scientific study of light got a big boost in 1665. English physicist and mathematician Isaac Newton (1643–1727)—most famous for discovering the law of **gravity**—used a prism to prove that sunlight was composed of seven different colors. He covered up all but one of the colors and shone it through a second prism. The beam was wider but still consisted of just the single color. Then he shone the entire spectrum through an upside-down prism, and it became a single beam of white light.

Newton also placed an obstacle between a source of light and a screen. The obstacle cast a shadow on the screen. He concluded that beams of light consisted of tiny particles, which the obstacle absorbed or deflected. The other particles had no trouble getting through to the screen and lighting it up.

A decade later, Danish astronomer Ole Roemer (1644–1710) found a method for calculating the speed of light. Like other astronomers of the era, he studied Jupiter's moons in their **orbits** around the giant planet. He noted that the time when the moons appeared and vanished changed throughout the year. Roemer thought the discrepancy arose because the distance between Jupiter and Earth varied during the moons' orbits. The farther away the two planets were from each other, the longer it took light from Jupiter's moons to travel here. He published his findings in 1676. Soon afterward, Dutch scientist Christiaan Huygens (1629–95) used Roemer's data to calculate the speed of light as 137,000 miles (220,480 km) per second.

In 1690, Huygens published the *Treatise on Light*, in which he contradicted Newton by saying that light was a series of waves rather than particles. Huygens pointed out that, when two beams of light crossed each other, each beam continued on its original path. If the beams consisted of particles, they should have collided with each other and been forced apart like streams of water coming from two hoses at an angle to each other.

English scientist Thomas Young (1773–1829) conducted an experiment in 1801

French physicist Léon Foucault in the 1850s

that supported Huygens's theory. Young directed a beam of light through a screen with two narrow slits. The light shone onto a second screen behind the first one. If light was composed of particles, Young reasoned, each slit should produce a similar narrow patch on the second screen. If light was a wave, like an ocean wave coming into a harbor through a narrow entrance, the beam would form a much wider pattern. His experiment revealed that wider pattern. Young also saw alternating light and dark bands of light, called interference patterns. Only waves could produce those bands.

The quest to determine the speed of light resumed in 1849, when French physicist Armand Fizeau (1819–96) aimed a beam of light through a gap in a rapidly spinning toothed wheel at a mirror several miles away. When it returned a fraction of a second later, the beam passed through the next gap. Using the distance between the gaps and the speed of the spinning wheel, Fizeau calculated the speed of light as 195,615 miles (314,812 km) per second.

The following year, fellow French physicist Léon Foucault (1819–68) designed an even more accurate apparatus. Small enough to fit on a tabletop, this tool used a series of stationary mirrors on a flat board to reflect a beam of light into a microscope. The mirrors generated a tiny shift in the path of the light, which Foucault measured. According to his measurement, the speed of light was 185,093 miles (297,878 km) per second. Sophisticated modern instruments using laser beams produce a virtually identical figure—186,282 miles (299,792 km) per second.

The wave theory received more support from Scottish mathematician James Clerk Maxwell (1831–79) in 1873. After a long series of calculations, Maxwell proved that electricity and magnetism were so similar that they needed to be called electromagnetism. He further proved that electromagnetic waves traveled at the speed of light. Therefore light itself was a type of electromagnetic wave.

There was just one problem with the wave theory. Sound waves need a medium such as air in order to travel. So do waves in water. Not unreasonably, scientists thought light

Scottish physicist James Clerk Maxwell, circa 1860s

waves also needed a medium to carry them. Many believed that medium was ether—a kind of "electric air"—even though they couldn't detect it.

In 1887, American physicists Albert Michelson (1852–1931) and Edward Morley (1838–1923) tried to prove ether's existence. They reasoned that ether should have some effect on Earth as it moved, like a swimmer in a river. Using a sensitive instrument called an interferometer, they split a beam of light into two parts. They sent one in the direction of Earth's orbital motion and the second at **right angles** to the first. If ether existed, it would interfere with the right-angled beam and slow it down. But no matter in which direction the beams were turned, their speeds remained identical. This meant there was no ether. Light and other electromagnetic waves didn't need any kind of medium. They could travel through the **vacuum** of outer space.

Some of the most important discoveries associated with light came from German-born physicist Albert Einstein (1879–1955).

Auroras are natural, electrical light displays

Einstein's special theory of relativity, published in 1905, was based on his conclusion that nothing could travel faster than the speed of light, which was absolute and didn't depend on the point of view of an observer. The closer someone came to the speed of light, the more time slowed down and the smaller objects would become. This theory brought Einstein into conflict with Newton, who had said that time and space were absolute and unchanging.

That same year, Einstein solved a riddle that had puzzled scientists for nearly two decades. They knew that a beam of light could generate an electric current—called the photoelectric effect—in metal sheets, but they didn't understand how it worked. Einstein said a stream of particles composed of tiny packets of energy called **photons** dislodged negatively charged electrons from the sheets and created the current. Einstein concluded that Newton and Huygens had both been correct. Sometimes light behaves as a particle, and at other times it behaves as a wave. This dual nature was difficult for physicists to accept, though.

Einstein also laid the groundwork for the development of lasers. In 1917, his calculations revealed the concept of stimulated emission of radiation, but no one followed up on it until **radar** was introduced during World War II (1939–45). American physicist Charles Townes (1915–) helped develop radar systems that guided American bombers to their targets. After the war, Townes worked to further improve radar systems by using microwaves because of their shorter wavelength. In 1951, he began experimenting with stimulated emission involving microwaves, and two years later he built the first maser ("microwave amplification by stimulated emission of radiation"). Townes and fellow American physicist Arthur Schawlow (1921–99) published a paper in 1958 showing how the principles of masers could extend to the visible light spectrum, though they didn't actually build a laser. Yet another American physicist, Theodore Maiman (1927–2007), is generally credited with building the first operational laser in 1960, thereby launching one of the most important light-related tools ever devised.

ANNALEN
DER
PHYSIK.

BEGRÜNDET UND FORTGEFÜHRT DURCH

F. A. C. GREN, L. W. GILBERT, J. C. POGGENDORFF, G. UND E. WIEDEMANN.

VIERTE FOLGE.

BAND 17.

DER GANZEN REIHE 322. BAND.

KURATORIUM:

**F. KOHLRAUSCH, M. PLANCK, G. QUINCKE,
W. C. RÖNTGEN, E. WARBURG.**

UNTER MITWIRKUNG

DER DEUTSCHEN PHYSIKALISCHEN GESELLSCHAFT

UND INSBESONDERE VON

M. PLANCK

HERAUSGEGEBEN VON

PAUL DRUDE.

MIT FÜNF FIGURENTAFELN.

Einstein published several papers in Europe's leading physics journal

EX·UMBRA·IN·SOLEM·

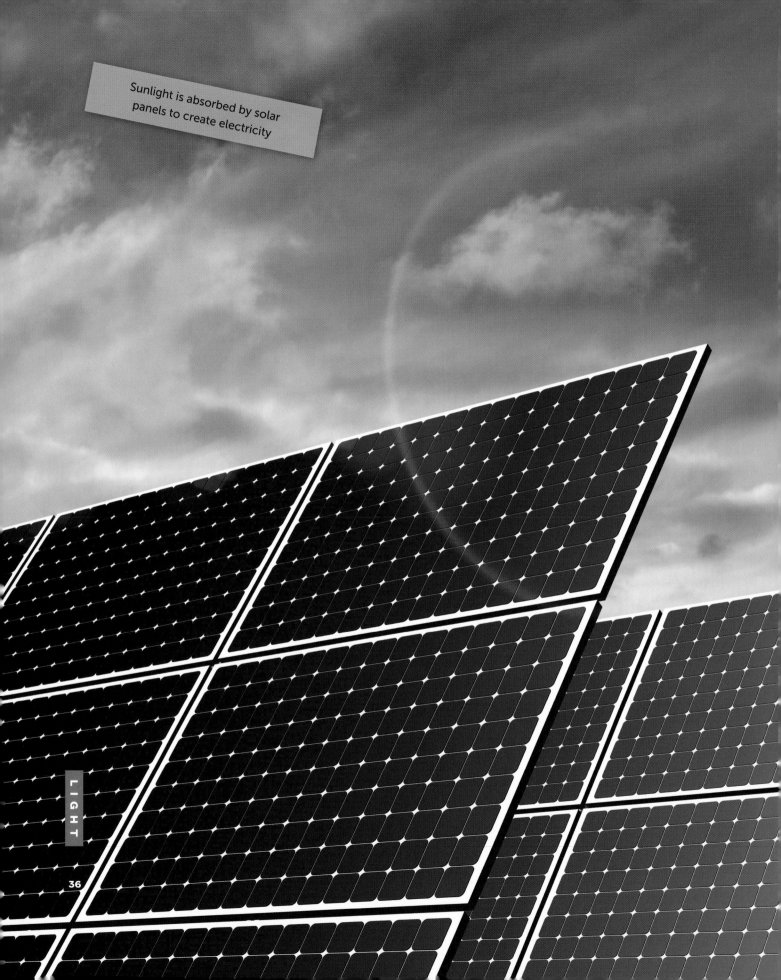

Sunlight is absorbed by solar panels to create electricity

THE FUTURE OF LIGHT

There is certainly no shortage of research being done on light and its related topics. Some of this research is being conducted with a sense of particular urgency. As the global population continues to grow and place ever-increasing demands on electricity, many scientists hope that solar power can provide an alternative to fossil fuels (such as coal and oil) and nuclear power. Sunlight costs nothing and is pollution-free, but the technology to harness and store it is expensive. Researchers hope to dramatically lower the cost over time by increasing technical capabilities.

Medical researchers are investigating ways in which light can help to combat serious diseases. For example, two of the deadliest forms of cancer are leukemia and T-cell lymphoma. Every year, these diseases combined kill more than 20,000 Americans, making them the sixth most common cause of cancer deaths in men and seventh among women. Recently a treatment called phototherapy has given hope of decreasing the death toll. Patients are given a chemical compound called psoralen, which breaks down the **DNA** in diseased cells. Then the patient's blood is pumped out of the body through plastic tubing and exposed to intense UV light before being pumped back in. Ongoing research seeks to test the value of the procedure and identify any potential side effects.

Lasers already play a vital role in medicine, and further research is likely to make them even more valuable. In 1999, a team of surgeons and researchers at Vanderbilt University's Free-Electron Laser (FEL) Center pioneered the use of lasers in brain surgery, an increasingly common procedure today. Lasers cut away dangerous brain tumors with a precision and sharpness conventional steel scalpels can't match. Some physicians speculate that lasers are capable of even more delicate operations, such as curing mental disorders by the application of low-power laser light, which can cause beneficial chemical reactions that restore proper functioning to the brain. For all their advances, though, medical researchers are unlikely to find a "cure" for Autosomal Dominant Compelling Helio-Ophthalmic Outburst Syndrome, which may afflict 20 to 30 percent of the American population. Also known as ACHOO, this condition means that suddenly emerging into bright sunlight can make you sneeze!

Laser usage will likely extend into many fields besides medicine, such as exploring the deepest reaches of the universe. In the 1400s and 1500s, European explorers came to the Americas in ships powered by the wind in their sails. Some scientists are proposing a revival of sail power as humans begin contemplating exploring the vast new worlds of interstellar travel. Leik Myrabo, an aerospace engineering professor at New York's Rensselaer Polytechnic Institute, has tested laser beams directed at lightweight sails on small experimental vehicles. These vehicles have risen more than 200 feet (61 m) into the air. (While this may not seem like much, it's about the same height that early rockets reached in the 1920s.)

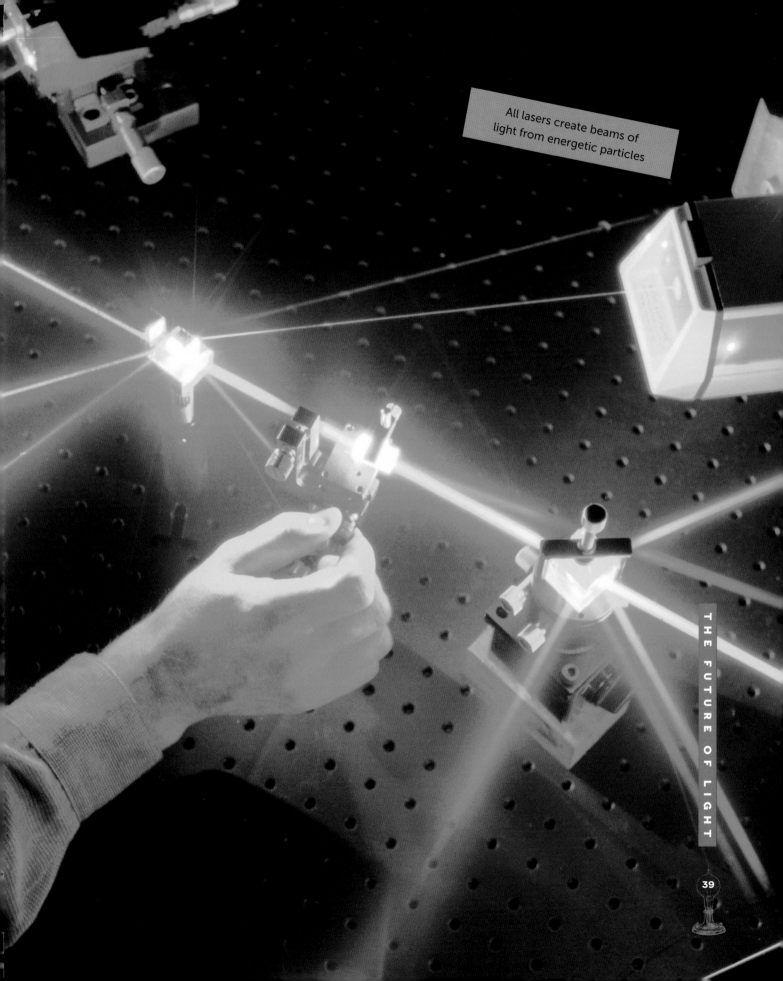

All lasers create beams of
light from energetic particles

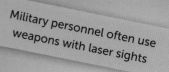

Military personnel often use weapons with laser sights

The Name Is Bond—Laser Bond

The James Bond films are famous for the gadgets Agent 007 uses, and at least six include laser devices, some of which are used by Bond and others which are used against him. The most famous 007 laser scene comes in *Goldfinger* (1964), as Bond is tied to a metal table. He watches in horror as a laser beam slices through the table and makes its way toward him. Supervillain Ernst Blofeld, Bond's archenemy, builds a laser weapon in outer space in *Diamonds Are Forever* (1971) and uses it to attack American, Chinese, and Russian nuclear weapons facilities. In *Moonraker* (1979), Bond uses a laser in a space station to blast apart containers carrying deadly nerve gas before they can enter Earth's atmosphere. He utilizes a wristwatch laser in both *Never Say Never Again* (1983) and *Goldeneye* (1995). In *The Living Daylights* (1987), the British spy makes use of a hubcap-mounted laser to wreck a pursuing police car. Especially in the early films, the filmmakers may have exaggerated the capability of lasers. At the time of *Goldfinger*, for instance, laser technology was in its infancy, and industrial lasers capable of cutting through metal didn't yet exist. The effect came from a welding torch located beneath the table.

Within our solar system, sunlight might power such a spacecraft. Then lasers mounted on the spacecraft could take over, delivering a concentrated beam of energy to the sails that would easily push the vehicle because there would be no atmospheric resistance to slow it down.

The darker side of laser technology is that it can be used to create instruments of destruction. From the moment lasers were introduced, the United States and other countries have been interested in developing laser-based weaponry. Today, the militaristic possibilities for laser applications include shooting down enemy aircraft (traveling at the speed of light, they wouldn't give their targets any time for evasive maneuvers), using them as rangefinders (devices that calculate the distance to a potential target), and communicating with submerged submarines. The best-known potential military use of lasers is for the U.S.'s Strategic Defense Initiative (SDI), nicknamed "Star Wars" because it seems so futuristic. SDI's intent is to find incoming enemy missiles and destroy them long before they reach their targets. Satellite-mounted lasers would detect the missiles, which would then be destroyed by intense laser beams or smaller missiles guided to the target by lasers. The system is costly, and there are serious questions about the value of continuing its development, though.

Not all light-related research is directed at improving contemporary technology. Through a series of experiments that began in the mid-1990s, Dr. Lene Hau, a physicist at Harvard University, has succeeded in dramatically reducing the speed of light. As she once explained to *The Boston Globe*, the phenomenon represents a "new territory, a new regime of nature." Using a laser, Hau cooled a cloud of sodium atoms to a billionth of a degree above absolute zero (-459 °F, or -273 °C), the point at which scientists believe no further cooling is possible. Then she used an electromagnet to suspend the cloud in a vacuum chamber, where it changed into a molasses-like goop. A light pulse fired into the frigid mass immediately got bogged down and slowed to the speed of someone riding a bicycle. In some experiments, Hau even succeeded in bringing light to a complete stop for a fraction of a second.

It's not clear what practical applications Hau's work may have, but such considerations don't seem important right now. She noted that Charles Townes initially thought that the laser—to which he contributed the theoretical framework—would simply be a way of correcting typos on manual typewriters. And as Hau explained, "sitting there late at night in the lab, and knowing light is going at bicycle speed, and that nobody in the history of mankind has ever been here before—that is mind-boggling. It's worth everything." In other words, discovering something is often its own reward, especially at first.

Light plays an important role in one of the most interesting phenomena in the universe—black holes. Black holes form when massive stars exhaust their supply of hydrogen, which produces immense amounts of heat and light as it burns in the star's core. Without hydrogen, the star's gravity collapses the star into a tiny bit of matter under tremendous pressure. The inward pressure of gravity is so strong that nothing, not even light, can escape. Black holes were discovered in the 1960s, and many of

Black holes don't emit light but can still be detected by other means

43

A Better Way of Lighting?

Electric lighting systems gobble up more than six percent of all energy produced worldwide—and much more than that in the U.S. and Canada. One possible solution to this dilemma is solid-state lighting (SSL), which could reduce energy consumption by 50 percent or more while lasting much longer than existing lighting systems. In 2007, the U.S. Department of Energy's Office of Energy Efficiency and Renewable Energy designated Sandia National Laboratories as the lead laboratory to research this new technology. SSL uses light-emitting **diodes** (LEDs). Sandia researchers hope to develop low-cost ways of combining existing diodes to produce white light or to discover new technologies that would achieve the same objective. The ultimate goal is to develop SSL to the point where it becomes not only cost-effective but also completely environmentally friendly by 2020. Yet reducing energy demands may not be the end result of Sandia's research. "Presented with the availability of cheaper light, humans may use more of it, as has happened over recent centuries with remarkable consistency following other lighting innovations," said lead researcher Jeff Tsao. "That is, rather than functioning as an instrument of decreased energy use, LEDs may be instead the next step in increasing human productivity and quality of life."

their mysteries have yet to be revealed. One difficulty in studying them, of course, is that they don't emit any light, making them nearly impossible to see. One of the best methods of detecting them is through X-ray telescopes, such as the Chandra X-ray Observatory, operated by the National Aeronautics and Space Administration (NASA). Launched into orbit in 1999, Chandra has revealed a wealth of information about black holes and other celestial phenomena.

All these and other types of research may finally solve the ultimate riddle about what light is. Because light has properties of both particles and waves, some people combine the two words and call light a wavicle. As **neuroscientist** Kyle Kirkland notes in his book *Light and Optics*, "Only time will tell whether people will continue to regard light as waves and particles, or whether people will finally achieve a deeper, and perhaps more satisfying, understanding of the nature of light."

One thing, though, is abundantly clear. Light is essential for everything we do. Whether directly or indirectly, sunlight provides the energy for our activities, and both natural and artificial light give us ways of knowing the world around us that our ancestors could only dream about. And in the form of lasers or some other technology, light will ultimately allow us to probe the farthest reaches of our universe.

ENDNOTES

acronym — a word formed from the first letters of other words

astronomers — people engaged in the scientific study of planets, stars, and other celestial phenomena

atom — the smallest part of an element with the chemical properties of that element

diodes — electronic components with two terminals, or connection points, that conduct an electrical current in a single direction

DNA — deoxyribonucleic acid; the substance that carries genetic information from parents to their offspring

electromagnetic spectrum — the range of wavelengths produced by electrical and magnetic currents in space that carry energy

electromagnetic waves — waves produced by the motion of electrically charged particles

filament — a slender fiber or wire with a high melting point that is heated in an electric blub

galaxy — a system of stars held together by mutual gravitational attraction and separated from similar systems by vast regions of space

gamma rays — the shortest waves on the electromagnetic spectrum; they can be generated by radioactive materials and nuclear explosions

gravity — the force of attraction between all masses in the universe that causes objects to fall toward the center of the earth, and which keeps the moon in steady orbit around Earth and the planets in orbit around the sun

hematologist — a physician who treats blood diseases and disorders

Hubble Space Telescope — a powerful telescope launched into Earth orbit in 1990, which is estimated to remain in service until 2013

incandescent — producing light when a source of heat is applied

molecules — combinations of two or more atoms bound together

nanometers — units of measurement equal to one billionth of a meter

neuroscientist — a scientist who studies the nervous system and brain

optical illusion — an image perceived as differing from objective reality; it often consists of distortions of line, color, and/or shape that fool the eyes and brain

orbits — curved paths that celestial objects take around a larger celestial object

paleontologist — a person who studies prehistoric life forms

photons — units of light energy that have wavelengths but no mass

physicist — a person who studies matter and motion through space and time in an effort to discover the physical laws of the universe

prisms — transparent optical devices with a triangular base and rectangular sides that show the seven colors of visible light when a beam is introduced into one side

radar — acronym for "radio detection and ranging"; the system involves sending out radio waves and timing their return if they strike an object to determine the object's distance and direction

radiation — the giving off of energy as electromagnetic waves or as particles smaller than atoms

radio waves — the longest waves on the electromagnetic spectrum; they can be used for communicating in radio, television, and cell phones

refraction — the change in direction, due to traveling at different speeds, that light rays undergo when they pass from one medium into another (such as from air into water)

right angles — angles formed by the perpendicular intersection of two straight lines

science fiction — a type of fiction writing in which scientific principles or discoveries play an important role

vacuum — a space from which air has been removed

WEB SITES

Amazing Space: The Star Witness News
http://amazing-space.stsci.edu/news/
Keep up with all the latest "tele-scoops" from the Hubble Space Telescope through this online newspaper.

Ask an Astrophysicist: X-ray/Gamma Ray Astronomy
http://imagine.gsfc.nasa.gov/docs/ask_astro/xrays.html
Get all your electromagnetic spectrum questions answered here, and find new resources for further research.

SELECTED BIBLIOGRAPHY

Advameg, Inc. Science Clarified. "Science and Technology: Lasers." http://www.scienceclarified.com/scitech/Lasers/index.html.

Baker, Joanne. *50 Physics Ideas You Really Need to Know*. London: Quercus Publishing, 2007.

Bova, Ben. *The Story of Light*. Naperville, Ill.: Sourcebooks, 2001.

Burnie, David. *Eyewitness Science: Light*. New York: Dorling Kindersley, 1992.

Chown, Marcus. *The Quantum Zoo: A Tourist's Guide to the Neverending Universe*. Washington, D.C.: Joseph Henry Press, 2006.

Hawking, Stephen. *The Illustrated A Brief History of Time*. New York: Bantam Books, 1996.

Kirkland, Kyle. *Light and Optics*. New York: Facts on File, 2007.

Waldman, Gary. *Introduction to Light: The Physics of Light, Vision, and Color*. Mineola, N.Y.: Dover Publications, 2002.

McLEAN COUNTY UNIT #5
105-CARLOCK

INDEX

ancient cultures and light 17
  sun worship 17
  theories 17
astronomers 10, 18
atoms 9, 14, 24, 34, 42
  combined as molecules 14
  particles of 34
Autosomal Dominant Compelling
    Helio-Opthalmic Outburst
    Syndrome 38
black holes 42, 44
Bova, Ben 24
camera obscura 21
chlorophyll 14
Edison, Thomas 23
Einstein, Albert 32, 34
  photoelectric effect 34
  theory of special relativity 34
electromagnetic radiation 10, 13–14,
    24, 30, 32, 34, 37
  gamma rays 13
  infrared 13
  radio waves 13
  ultraviolet 13–14, 24, 37
  visible light 13, 24, 34
  wave measurement 13, 24
  X-rays 14
energy 14, 37
  fossil fuels 37
  nuclear power 37
  solar power 37
ether 32
five senses 10
Fizeau, Armand 30
Foucault, Léon 30
galaxies 15
  Andromeda 15
Galileo Galilei 18, 21
gravity 29, 42
Hau, Lene 42
Huygens, Christiaan 29, 30, 34
  Treatise on Light 29
interferometers 32
James Bond films 41

and use of lasers 41
Kelvin, William Thomson, 1st Baron
  9
Kirkland, Kyle 44
  Light and Optics 44
light, properties 9, 10, 13, 14, 18, 21,
    23, 24, 27, 29, 30, 32, 34, 44
  colors 13, 14, 29
  interference patterns 30
  particles 29, 30, 34, 44
  refraction 18, 21
  waves 29, 30, 32, 34, 44
light sources 10, 13, 14, 15, 17, 23–24,
    29, 37, 44, 45
  electricity 10, 14, 23–24, 37, 44
  fires 10, 17
  stars 10, 15
  sun 10, 13, 14, 15, 17, 29, 37, 45
light, speed 9, 14–15, 17, 18, 29, 30,
    34, 41, 42
light technology 18, 21, 23–24, 27, 30,
    34, 37, 38, 41–42, 44, 45
  fluorescent lighting 23–24
  lasers 24, 27, 30, 34, 37, 38, 41–42,
    45
  lens making 18, 21
  light bulbs 23, 24
  microscopes 21, 30
  optical fibers 27
  phototherapy cancer treatments
    37
  solid-state lighting 44
  sunlight-powered spacecraft 38,
    41
light years 15
Lippershey, Hans 21
Maiman, Theodore 34
  first laser 34
Massachusetts Institute of
    Technology 27
  "Luna See" project 27
matter 42
Maxwell, James Clerk 30
Michelson, Albert 9, 32

moon 10, 27
Morley, Edward 32
Myrabo, Leik 38
NASA 44
Newton, Isaac 29, 34
orbits 29, 32, 44
photography 21
planets 29
Proxima Centauri 15
rainbows 13
Rensselaer Polytechnic Institute 38
Roemer, Ole 29
Sandia National Laboratories 44
Schawlow, Arthur 34
science fiction 24
space and time 34
Strategic Defense Initiative 41
telescopes 15, 21, 23, 27, 44
  Chandra X-ray Observatory 44
  Hubble Space Telescope 23
  X-ray 44
Townes, Charles 34, 42
  first maser 34
Tron 27
Tron: Legacy 27
Tsao, Jeff 44
Vanderbilt University 37
  Free-Electron Laser Center 37
World War II 34
  invention of radar 34
Young, Thomas 29–30